TICKLE YO... ...IN

Roman Riot!

First published in the UK in 2011 by The Salariya Book Company Ltd
This edition published in the UK in 2024 by Hatch Press,
an imprint of Bonnier Books UK
4th Floor, Victoria House
Bloomsbury Square, London WC1B 4DA
Owned by Bonnier Books
Sveavägen 56, Stockholm, Sweden
www.bonnierbooks.co.uk

1 3 5 7 9 10 8 6 4 2

ISBN 978-1-80078-849-7

Printed in the United Kingdom

MIX
Paper | Supporting
responsible forestry
FSC
www.fsc.org
FSC® C018072

TICKLE YOUR BRAIN
FACTS AND JOKES

Roman Riot!

Hatch

INTRODUCTION

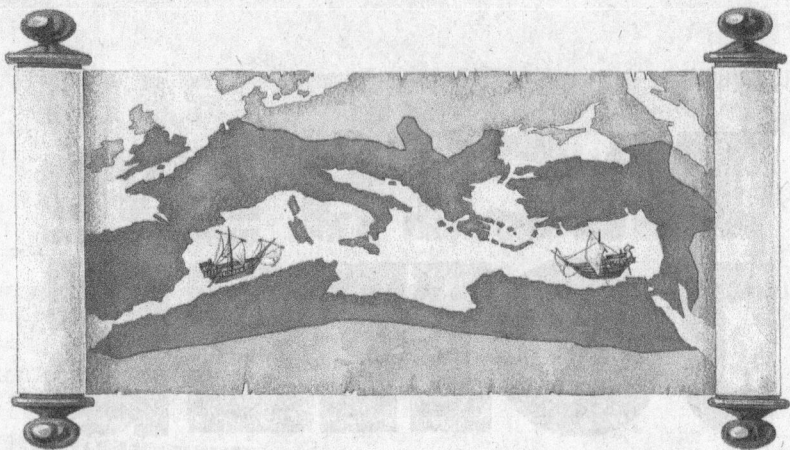

Welcome to the riotous world of ancient Rome! This hilarious book covers every aspect of Roman history in Britain, tracing their impact across the Isles. Get ready to uncover gory details from brutal battles and ferocious emperors to back-stabbing plots and courageous Celts. It's time to put on your sandals, grab your toga, and tickle your brain!

The ancient Romans really were an impressive bunch. Their legacy stretches across the British Isles, and the world at large, to this very day. As expert innovators and civil engineers, they created many inventions that changed the globe. They developed concrete, modern roads, aqueducts, baths and even underfloor heating. They even crafted a legal and political system that still lays the groundwork for much of the world today. No wonder they're so popular!

**With the Romans, we've all
become smitten,
As so many books have
been written,
But none like this one,
(Which is second to none),
For learning about
Romans in Britain!**

THE ROMAN EMPIRE

The great Roman Empire started in 753 BC and lasted for over 1,000 years. During that time, Rome grew to rule much of Europe, Western Asia and Northern Africa. The Romans had a lasting impact across the world, where Roman remains, objects and buildings are still being uncovered.

Rome first emerged as a powerhouse whilst it was still a Republic. This meant that Rome was ruled by elected officials that served for a limited amount of time – unlike kings who inherited power.

This all changed in 45 BC when Julius Caesar took over and declared himself supreme dictator, ending the Republic. After his assassination, Caesar Augustus would take control in 27 BC and become the very first Emperor. As the Empire grew, it sprawled across the globe and eventually split in two: the Western Empire and the Eastern (or Byzantine) Empire.

The Roman Empire finally fell in 476 AD when the final Emperor (Romulus Augustus) was defeated by the German Goth Odoacer — and 'the Dark Ages' in Europe began...

Who'd like more flamingo trifle?

IN THE BEGINNING...

Clear off!

Before the Romans arrived, Britain was inhabited by scattered Celtic tribes. There were no towns or proper roads – the Celts mainly lived in small farming settlements. No one really knows where they came from, or when exactly, but they are thought to have come over from Central Europe a very long time ago...

The word Celt comes from the Greek word, *Keltoi*, which means barbarians, and is pronounced as 'Kelt'. The Romans usually called them Britons and described them like this:

'They are very tall in stature, with rippling muscles under clear white skin. Their hair is blond, but not naturally so: they bleach it, to this day, artificially, washing it in lime and combing it back from their foreheads. They look like wood-demons, their hair thick and shaggy like a horse's mane. Some of them are clean-shaven, but others – especially those of high rank – shave their cheeks but leave a moustache that covers the whole mouth.'

Diodorus Siculus (A Roman historian)

BRUTAL BRITONS!

From Rome, Britain was far across the sea with her own tempting gold and tin. The Romans just couldn't resist – they would go on to invade and rule much of the nation for 400 years.

But before thousands of Roman soldiers arrived in 43 AD, the Celtic Brits occupied the land. They were terrifying warriors and tribesmen – they banded together to fight the Romans just as often as they fought each other! Julius Caesar described the native Britons as a rowdy rabble who 'dye themselves with woad*, which occasions a bluish colour, and thereby have a more terrible appearance in fight. They wear their hair long, and have every part of their body shaved except their head and upper lip.'

*woad = a plant of the cabbage family, grown in ancient Britain for making blue dye.
The Romans referred to Ancient Britons as 'Picts', which is Celtic for painted or tattooed.

Blue is definitely my colour!

Although there is no concrete evidence that the Britons actually dyed their bodies blue, it certainly paints a frightening picture! Caesar believed that the Brits painted themselves to intimidate rivals in battle, though they may have been tattoos. Research suggests it was custom among certain groups, like 'the Picts', to adorn their bodies with symbols and colours specific to their tribe.

ROMANS ON THE MOVE

The Roman Army was always being sent off to conquer new lands. Soldiers were well-paid but it was a tough life — especially when they marched to hostile places far from home, like Britain. In fact, it took three attempts for the Romans to conquer Britain. Julius Caesar tried to invade twice, in 55 BC and the following year. His ships were wrecked in storms and, when they eventually landed on the Kent coast, they had to fight the local 'barbarian' Brits.

Deterred by Britain's determined Celtric tribes, it would take nearly 100 years before the Romans dared to return again and try another invasion. This time was more successful...

In 43 AD, Emperor Claudius sent 40,000 soldiers across the English Channel, even though many were terrified. The full might of the Roman army landed on the beaches in Kent and began battling inland, chopping down anyone who stood in their way. The Romans wanted Britain's precious metals. They called the land 'Britannia', which meant 'land of tin'. As they spread through the country, they built forts, new towns and roads. They also spread their culture, laws, language – and public toilets.

WATCH YOUR LANGUAGE

Before the Romans conquered the British Isles, most Celts couldn't read or write. The two major spoken languages were Goidelic in Ireland and Brittonic in present-day Wales, England and parts of Scotland. But when the Romans did arrive, they introduced Latin and writing. Events were written down and recorded in Latin; these words began to shape communication around the Isles. Even today, 2,000 years later, many of our common phrases stem from the Romans – particularly words related to warfare or government. Some surprising terms we've borrowed include 'decimate', 'victory' and 'triumph'; 'dictator' and 'consul'; and even 'circus' which referred to public spectacles in ancient Rome.

JOKE TIME

When the Romans arrived
from warm Italy,
They complained of the cold
very bitterly,
Turning blue as they strode...
'It's the end of the woad!'
Laughed the blue-painted Britons,
so wittily.

Q: When the Roman Emperor asked what
weather to expect in Britain, what did they
say?

A: 'Hail, Caesar.' (Or maybe 'There'll be an
awful lot of reigning!')

Q: When the Romans first arrived in Britain, how do we know they often got lost?

A: Because the Britons found them Roman (roamin') all over the place.

Q: What did the ancient Britons say when the Romans arrived?

A: Don't lat-in that lot! (Actually, ancient Britons didn't speak English – but yes, the Romans spoke and wrote in Latin.)

Q: What ships did the ancient Romans use?

A: DictatorSHIPS!

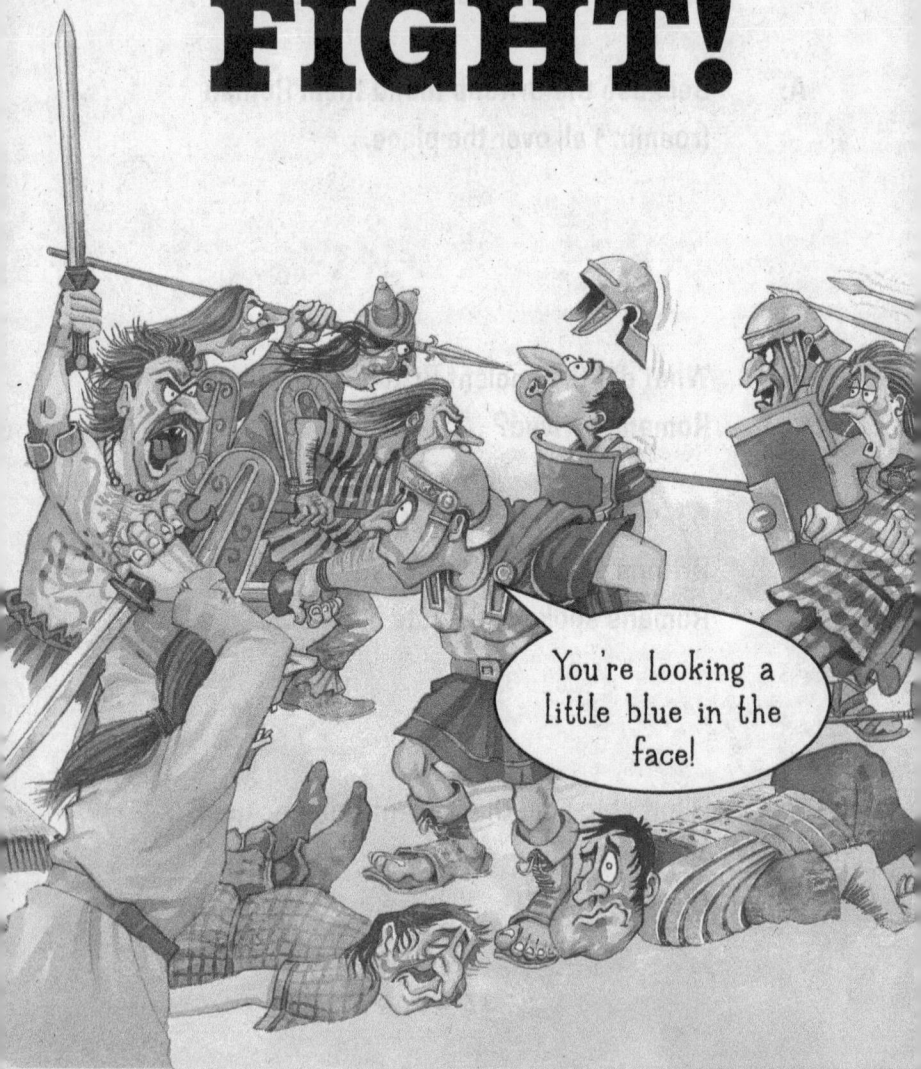

When the Romans invaded, they battled cut-throat Celtic tribes, determined to defend their land. In 60 AD, one native leader raised a huge army. She was Queen Boudicca of the Iceni tribe. Her forces rampaged Roman towns, burning Colchester and London before heading north to St Albans. When the Roman army heard about this, they abandoned their campaign in Wales to face Boudicca. Even though the Romans were outnumbered by Boudicca's 200,000 warriors, they were the better trained and better equipped side. Both sides clashed in a fierce battle, but the Romans finally won out. Romans 1, Britons 0. Boudicca dead. No one truly knows what happened to her; whether she killed herself to avoid capture, or died from illness.

ARRGGH

CAN YOU BELIEVE IT?

About 70,000–80,000 Romans and British were killed in the battles led by Boudicca. All this trouble made Emperor Nero consider withdrawing all Roman forces from Britain. But once Boudicca was out of the way, the Romans carried on invading more areas.

No GPS needed – all roads lead to Rome!

Most Britons in southern Britain settled down to Roman order and discipline. Towns grew up across the country, including York, Chester, St. Albans, Bath, Lincoln, Gloucester and Colchester. All of these major centres are still linked today by roads built by the Romans, radiating from the port of London. The Romans were now here to stay.

BY THE WAY – A NOTE ON NERO

(Emperor from 54 to 68 AD)

A few Roman emperors were totally bonkers. Nero was one of them. He didn't like his mother much so he tried to poison her – three times. Each time he failed so it was Plan B. He made the ceiling collapse on her. She survived. Plan C was to sink the ship she was sailing on. She survived. In the end, he fell back on his lethal last resort; he sent his own soldiers to stab her to death. What a lovely son!

NASTY NERO

But Nero's reign of terror didn't end with his mother. Oh no – he also had a nasty habit of turning Christians into human candles and burning them alive! Under Nero's rule, Christians became public enemy number one, as their new religion threatened the stability of the Roman Empire. The notorious Nero presided over a very tumultuous period of rule, including Boudicca's rebellion and the Great Fire of Rome that raged through the city for six days. But some modern historians have questioned Nero's villainous reputation, suggesting the man behind the myth was less monstrous than sources would have us believe.

Q: Did you hear about the rule of Nero?
A :   I heard it was a pretty lit time!

Q: Which Roman never gets asked out on a date?
A: Hidius!

GORY GLADIATORS

Gladiators were armed fighters (from the Latin word *gladius* for sword), who fought against each other, condemned criminals and wild animals. In most cases, they fought till one of them accepted defeat or was killed. Gladiators fought for the entertainment of the public.

People filled a stadium or amphitheatre to cheer on the gladiators fighting to the death in the arena. Those with ringside seats would risk getting splashed with blood, but that was all part of the fun, so they thought.

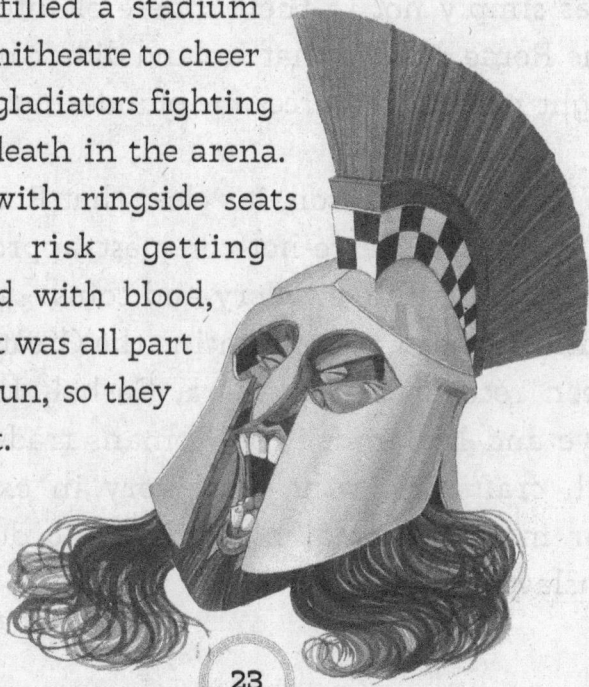

INVINCIBLE IRELAND

Surprisingly, the Romans never got around to conquering the Emerald Isle. In fact, they didn't even try. Maybe they were too busy dealing with the tribal uprisings in England, Wales and Scotland to be tempted by Hibernia – one of the Latin names for Ireland. Perhaps it was simply not in their sphere of interest, or the Rome decided that Ireland didn't have the right natural resources for plundering.

Whatever the reason, it's clear that Rome took a more commerce-not-conquest approach to Ireland. Roman jewellery and coins – adorned with the head of Containtine the Great – have been recovered from Tara, Cashel, Ireland's Eye and Malahide. The Romans traded olive oil, craftware, wine and ivory in exchange for metals, animal hides, hunting dogs and enslaved people.

DID YOU KNOW?

The most famous Roman slave to arrive in Ireland was St Patrick. Originally from Britain, he was stolen by pirates at age sixteen and carried to Ireland. He was enslaved for six long years before he finally escaped. His fortunes would change however, as he went on to become Ireland's patron saint and national apostle.

The only one getting through is the pizza delivery man!

WALES

If there's one thing the Romans couldn't stand, it was a Druid. A Druid was a priest or magician in the ancient Celtic religion. There were quite a few Druids in Wales, so the Romans went after them. A grisly attack on the island of Anglesey in 60 AD wiped out most of the Druids there. It was one of the most gruesome campaigns undertaken by the Romans in Britain. Men, women and children were ruthlessly killed, while Druid priests and their followers were thrown into ditches and burned alive.

At Caerleon – or Isca as it was known in Roman times – visitors today can see the amphitheatre and imagine all that blood and gore where gladiators and beasts fought tooth and claw. Down the Roman road is Venta Silurum, the first town in Wales and the tribal capital of the Silures – Caerwent today. It still has the remains of shops, a temple and the forum-basilica (a meeting place and marketplace).

Q: Why did the Romans find algebra so easy?
A :   Because the 'X' always equals 10!

Q: Can you make a good Caesar salad?
A: No – but I can give it a good stab!

Q: Who cares about learning the Roman Numeral system?
A :   I, for one...

SCOTLAND

The Romans were desperate to head to the far north of Britain to the land known as Caledonia (now called Scotland). The Roman Governor of Britain, called Agricola, tried to conquer Scotland in 79 AD, but the fearsome Picts wouldn't have it. By then, Rome ruled most of southern Britain — but Scotland was a much wilder place. It was still controlled by fierce warrior tribes who refused to bow to the Roman Empire.

Scotland had valuable silver and gold that the Romans wanted to mine. They also wanted to charge the people taxes and force them into slavery. But the powerful Scottish tribes had other ideas. In 84 AD, Caledonian tribes joined forces and made a stand against the invading Roman army. The two sides fought in the Grampian Mountains. The Picts had 30,000 warriors, about twice as many as the Romans.

Even so, the Romans were better organised and swiftly defeated the tribes. Romans 1, Picts 0. That wouldn't be the end though...

The Picts were a very resistant bunch. They refused to surrender, deploying guerilla warfare tactics and raiding the Roman forts with ruthless efficiency. They stole cattle, captured slaves and wreaked havoc. It was time for Rome to get tough – the Roman Emperor would come down on them with the full force of his power. "I'm going to build a wall!" he declared in his very best Latin. (Ego aedificare murum!)

"Go forth and build me a wall"

The Emperor was called Hadrian. You may have heard of him. He ruled for 21 years from 117 AD until 138 AD, when the Empire of Ancient Rome reached great heights (and soon, his wall would too). He planned to build a great wall that stretched across the north of England to keep out the pesky Picts and finally put a stop to their brutal raids.

FAST FACTS
Hadrian's Wall Edition

1 Hadrian's Wall was 117 km (73 miles) long, 2-3 metres (6.5-10 feet) wide, and took 6 years to build.

2 Many soldiers and their families lived in settlements right beside the wall.

3 In 197 AD the wall was overrun by the barbarian Picts from the north. Many of the forts had to be rebuilt.

4 Hadrian's Wall is still intact today in many places. It is a tourist attraction and you can walk along much of its length.

5 The wall required some serious manpower to build. It was worked on by three legions of around 5,000 infantrymen each. That's 15,000 in total!

TALKING IN TABLETS

Thin slices of oak have been found with Latin messages on them – each about the size of a postcard. These are known as the Vindolanda tablets, letters sent home from soldiers or to Roman officers serving at Vindolanda, Northumberland from 90 AD to 120 AD – just before Hadrian built his wall nearby.

Q: Why were Roman roads so straight?
A :   They were designed by their rulers!

Q: Why didn't they have smart phones in ancient Rome?
A: They didn't need them - they already had tablets!

The messages show what life was like for the Romans sent to garrisons in freezing, far-flung parts of the empire. Some officers pleaded for clothes to keep them warm through the Northumberland winter, including subuclae (vests) and abollae (thick heavy cloaks). 'Paria udonum ab Sattua solearum duo et subligariorum duo,' one soldier asks for. That's socks, two pairs of sandals and two pairs of underpants (no doubt extra thick!).

ROMAN VINDOLANDA

The Vindolanda tablets also show us what kind of food was eaten back then. Officers and other rich Romans enjoyed meats such as venison and wild boar. Other soldiers ate garlic, fish, semolina, lentils, olives, olive oil and the best Italian wine. The local Picts just ate pork fat, cereal and pork scratchings washed down with beer. Healthy eating wasn't top of their list.

One message home from a miserable Roman read: 'The British sky is obscured by constant rain and cloud.'

DID YOU KNOW?

The Romans in Britain weren't just men. Many Roman women lived in the camps along Hadrian's Wall. They were the wives, mothers, daughters and sisters of soldiers (even though ordinary soldiers weren't officially allowed to marry until 197 AD).

What did Spartacus say when the lion ate his wife? Nothing – he was glad-he-ate-her!

ROMAN HUMOUR

Teacher: Who can tell me where Hadrian's Wall is?

Pupil: Probably somewhere around Hadrian's garden, miss.

Teacher: The Celts had to choose their leaders carefully.

Pupil: They must have been hand-Pict.

Teacher: Archaeologists say that Roman cement was stronger in ancient times, than it is today.

Pupil: I'm yet to see any concrete evidence!

Q: What did the Roman workers say once they had completed another road?

A: We came, we saw, we concreted!

Q: What is the problem with Roman Lego?

A: You can't build it in a day!

Q: What was Emperor Hadrian's favourite brand of ice cream?

A: Walls!

ENGLAND

Five facts about Romans in England

1 The first Roman city in Britain was Camulodunum. Today it is the town of Colchester.

2 Many of today's cities in England were established by the Romans, including London, York, Northwich, Dover, Bath and Canterbury. Place names ending in 'cester', 'chester' or 'caster' were Roman forts or towns. How many can you name?

3 It was once thought that the Romans didn't settle much further west than Exeter in Devon, but recently Roman coins and other evidence found in Cornwall and Dartmoor suggests military camps here protected supply routes for tin.

You can also thank the Romans for bringing black rats over to Britain!

4 Towns in Roman Britain were small by today's standards. Colchester and Cirencester probably had between 10,000 and 12,000 people, but most towns were smaller with only 3,000–5,000 people.

5 Roman London was the biggest city Britain would see for over a thousand years. At around 120 AD, Londinium (as it was called) was home to about 45,000 people. It would not reach that size again until the 13th century.

BATH

The city of Bath in Somerset is famous for its – you guessed it! – Roman baths! Here, the hot spring water still bubbles naturally from the ground at 46°C (114°F). Back in the day, there was nothing the Romans liked better than hot water, taking a dip with friends and having a good scrub together. The Romans built bathhouses above Bath's three natural hot springs, beside a temple dedicated to the healing goddess Sulis-Minerva. The baths are now one of the best-preserved ancient Roman spas in the world.

Q: Why did the doctor tell the Roman soldier to go and take a bath?

A: He said he was feeling drained!

Bathtime at the Bath baths

A million litres of hot spring water burst each day from red-stained holes in the stone walls. Wafting up from the turquoise waters would be clouds of steam and sulphur fog. The sound of plunging soldiers, some cheering, some singing, would swirl in the hot, sticky mist. Other bathers were busy talking, laughing or scrubbing, some wrestling, and at the water's edge stalls sold sausages, oysters and roasted dormice. This type of scene attracted hordes of visitors to the famous baths, including emperors, soldiers, traders, housewives and children.

After a good scrape with a curved, metal tool called a *strigil*, used to scrub dirt and sweat from the body, bathers could have a warm bath in the tepidarium or plunge into a cold bath called the frigidarium. The cold water closed up the skin's pores again and got the blood flowing — to give a pleasant tingling feeling afterwards. Would you be tempted to try it?

Q:	Why did the Romans finally wash their hands of the Celts?

A:	They were a revolting lot!

Q:	What temperature did Julius Caesar like his bath water?

A:	Not too hot or cold – ROME temperature!

ROTTEN ROMANS

Despite their love for baths, scientists have found evidence of roundworms that lived inside Roman bodies, as well as parasites that lived outside the body — lice, fleas and bed bugs. This suggests that the Romans' bathhouses weren't keeping them much cleaner than Britons still living in their tribes in the forests. Yuck!

Anyone fancy a bath tonight?

IT GETS WORSE...

Archaeologists have discovered fine-toothed combs from the Roman period, probably used for removing lice from hair. Steamy bathhouses were ideal places for parasites to party. If the water wasn't changed very often, a scum from human dirt and gunge would spread over the surface – just right for microorganisms to breed. And another thing... parasites lived in human poo. What did the Romans do with human poo? They spread it on fields to feed plants and fertilise the soil. This is still done today in many places, and it is good for the plants... if you first compost the poo long enough to kill off any parasite eggs. But the Romans didn't know that. YUCK!

To their credit though, the Romans did clean up Britain by introducing sewers, plumbing, street cleaning and even public toilets. These bathrooms became, like the bathhouses, an integral part of communal life, where people would catch up as they went to the loo! Even so, just think of those scummy baths and the lurgies lurking within. Would you still be tempted to test the waters?

Did you watch the tennis match between Caligula and Nero?

Shocking result – it was refereed by the Roman Umpire!

SOME GROSS ROMAN FACTS

1

The inhabitants of ancient Rome had a sewer goddess, a toilet god and a god of excrement.

2

The Romans used powdered mouse brains as toothpaste – or even urine to whiten their teeth (just right for a wee smile). They also sloshed plenty of the warm liquid into their tubs when washing clothes. The ammonia in urine helped with cleaning, and pots were left outside shops and public urinals to collect public pee donations.

3

Life expectancy in Ancient Rome for many people was only about 20 to 30 years (not surprising if they spent much time in the public toilets).

The public toilets in Rome were often disgusting, likely never cleaned, and full of parasites. Romans using the toilets would have to take in special combs for scraping out lice from their skin and hair. The toilets were shared with lots of people, all sitting together, with just one sponge on a stick for passing round to wipe each bottom, without being washed in between. Nice.

Ergh – I've got hold of the wrong end of the stick.

LONDON

When the Romans arrived in Britain, the commander of troops was called Aulus Plautius. He marched his men from their landing place in Kent towards Colchester, their main base. There was only one issue: the whopping great river in the way! Plautius was forced to build a bridge to get his men across the River Thames. The Roman settlement grew on the north side of the bridge, called Londinium, which quickly became important as a trading centre for goods brought up the River Thames by boat and unloaded at wooden docks by the bridge. This first 'London Bridge' has been excavated and it's very close to the modern London Bridge.

The Romans found that the Picts and the River Thames had few things in common...
They were both pretty ex-stream – and neither could be Thamed!

I've come from Rome to see the bright lights of Londinium!

REMAINS IN THE MUD

Around the year 200 AD a wall was built all around the city to keep out enemies. For well over a millennium the shape and size of London was affected by this Roman wall. The area inside the is now 'the City', London's famous financial area. Traces of the wall can still be seen in a few places. But that's not all. Archaeologists have dug around in London clay for years and unearthed all kinds of Roman remains, including human bones.

Evidence of Roman Britain's slave trade has been unearthed here too: a receipt for a young French girl bought for the equivalent price of a small sports car today. Faint scratchings on a wooden writing tablet show that a wealthy household bought a girl named Fortunata (Lucky), a member of a Celtic tribe living in France. The tablet had been preserved in wet London soil for 2,000 years.

CAPTURED CELTS

The Romans captured many slaves in the countries they invaded. It was the same in Britain. Britons were forced to work in mines or on farms, with some given high status jobs like helping to run estates and households of wealthy Romans. In time, some slaves became rich enough to buy their own slaves – and their freedom. Others became soldiers. There were two kinds of Roman soldiers: legionaries – who were the best troops in the army – and auxiliaries, who were soldiers recruited in the lands conquered by the Romans.

Captured Celts were usually forced into manual labour, tasked with clearing forests, draining swamps, building roads and quarrying stone for all those Roman walls.

Look – someone's come to set us free!

Hmm, I smell a rat.

REVOLTING REMAINS

Scientists have studied skulls discovered at the London Wall, using the latest Crime Scene Science techniques at the Museum of London, where 39 skulls are kept. The skulls were discovered in 1988, in an industrial area known as the Upper Walbrook Valley in Roman times.

Finally landed my dream job as a gladiator. Will beheading to the arena tomorrow!

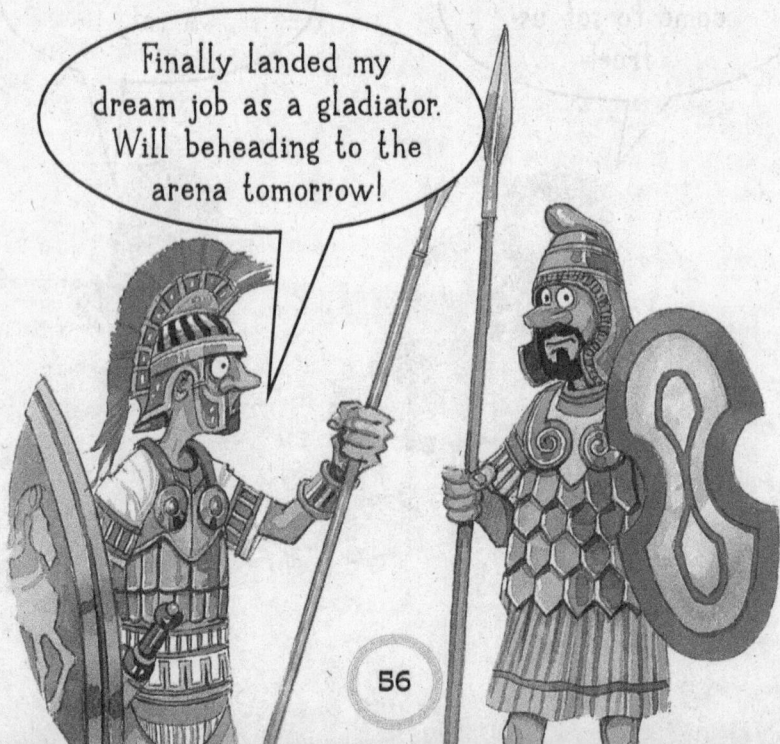

Despite the victims dying during peace time, historians have revealed that the skulls showed mutliple signs of violence before death. So why were so many severed heads of men buried in Roman London, and how did they meet such brutal ends? The experts have three possible answers...

Fallen gladiators

The most likely theory is that the men died in a local amphitheatre. Many of the violent injuries suggest that their death was caused by a brutal fight to the end, as was common among gladiators.

Executed criminals

Though gladiators often died in the ampitheatre, others could be beheaded there, too. The Roman ampitheatre was a place where common criminals were executed, or where criminals were forced to kill one another for entertainment. For many Romans, that made for a good day out.

THE FINAL THEORY...

Victims of head-hunting

The third theory is that the skulls are the heads of Scottish barbarians killed by Roman forces and brought to London as trophies. There is evidence of head-taking from across the Roman empire, and enemy heads have been depicted on the tombstones of British cavalry officers, held up in glorious victory. It would have taken many weeks to transport them from Scotland to London. And it certainly wouldn't have been a very pleasant ride, carrying a sack of smelly heads all that way!

As we say in Rome;
two heads are better
than one!

YORK

If anywhere captures the Roman's keen eye for locating the perfect spot for a fortress, it's York — or as it was known then, *Eboracum*. This major Roman city in the north of England rose up around 71 AD, after 5,000 soldiers of the Ninth Legion marched from Lincoln and set up camp there. They plonked their fortress on a slightly raised plateau nestled between the river Foss and the river Ouse, gaining a huge advantage on both sides.

Life's too fort for all this fighting!

York became a strategic Roman stronghold. It was used as a base to launch campaigns against sites of Brigantian resistance, hailing attacks down on the North York Moors and Pennine valleys. The fortress also provided great transport links. Positioned at the spot where both rivers joined, men and supplies could easily funnel in from the North Sea. Such a wealth of history makes York a dig come true for archaeologists; they've been unearthing gory details from our past here for centuries!

GRUESOME DISCOVERY

In an excavated area of York, archaeologists discovered 2,000-year-old remains of almost 80 young men. At first, it seemed the men were victims of a mass execution. Then scientists got to work and uncovered something incredible...

Shall we have an Italian tonight?

The men's injuries were vast and varied, ranging from severed heads to even tiger bites on at least one of the skeletons. This suggests that the bodies were likely gladiators who met a gruesome end entertaining the bloodthirsty crowds of the ancient world. Some skeletons showed healed injuries from weapons, suggesting frequent fights, and all men were described as tall and fit (despite, of course, being dead). Their skeletons showed signs of strong muscles, likely developed from weapons training. The men had suffered many injuries, including hammer blows to the head – a method popular among gladiators to finish off their opponents. York wasn't the only Roman city where gladiators fought to the death though...

Q: What happened to the two gladiator olives?
A: They were pitted against each other!

CHESTER

Other gruesome remains have been unearthed at an arena in Chester. In Roman times Chester was known as *Castra Deva*, meaning 'the military camp on the River Dee'. This town also saw grisly fights to the death for public entertainment.

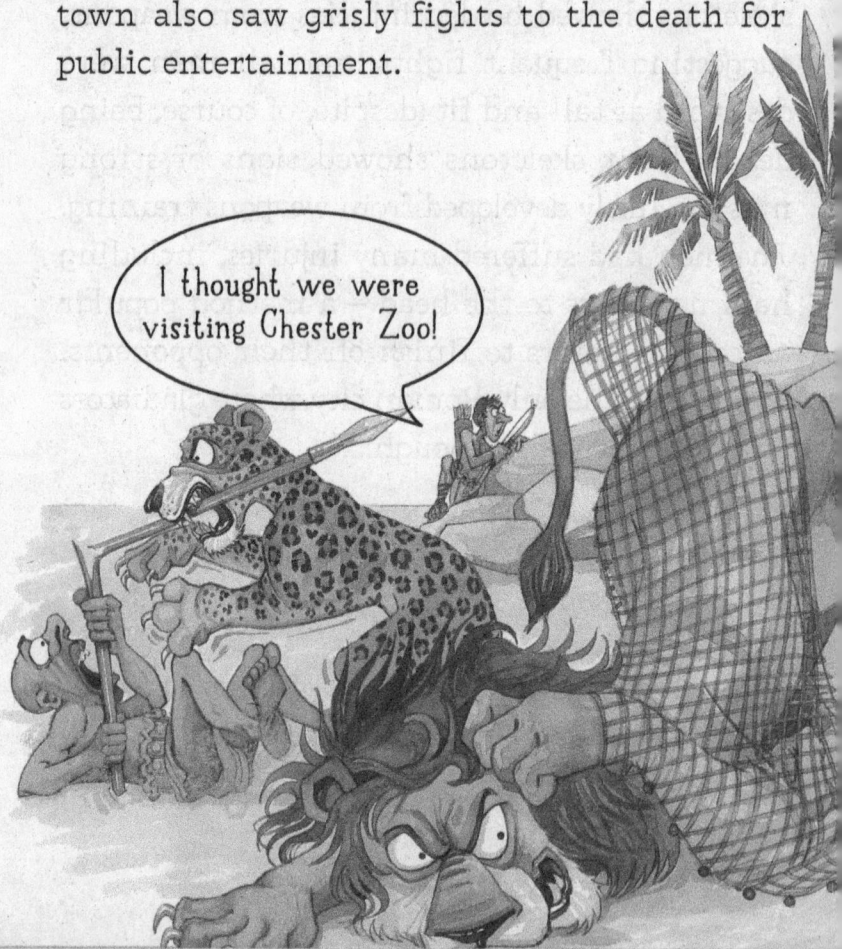

I thought we were visiting Chester Zoo!

A stone block with iron fittings was discovered at the centre of the two-storey amphitheatre, which dates to about 100 AD. Like other stone blocks found at the site, it was probably placed around the arena to prevent gladiators from sheltering against the walls and blocking a good view of the action. Chaining victims to these blocks was thought to be more fun for the audience — but grim for the gladiators!

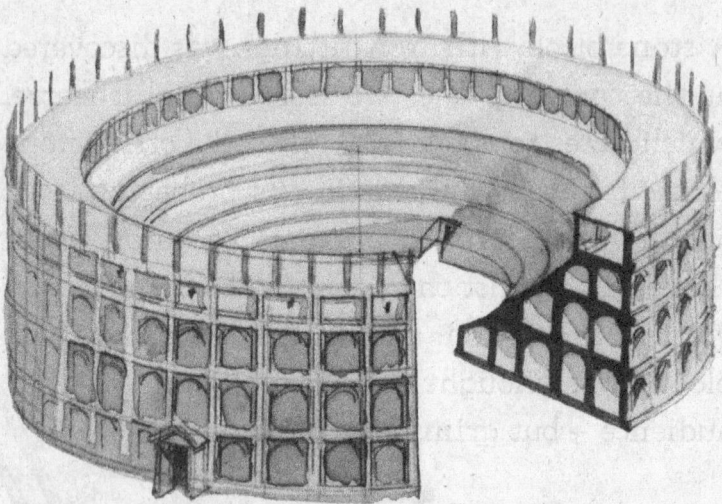

Archaeologists cannot be sure exactly what types of gladiator entertainment went on in Chester, but they believe it was most likely a type involving bestiaries (gladiators trained to fight savage animals). Interestingly, the Chester amphitheatre was rebuilt about 100 years after it was first used – redesigned to resemble a scaled-down version of Rome's grand Colosseum.

DID YOU KNOW?

There were female gladiators (gladiatrix or gladiatrices) in Ancient Rome. Although they were very rare, written records and archaeological evidence shows they did exist. They probably entertained the crowds in Britain, too. Archaeologists from the Museum of London believe they discovered the first known burial site of a female Roman gladiator in Southwark, south London. She had been cremated and given a special funeral. Maybe she was a big star of her time.

I'm a celebrity – get me out of here!

AND ANOTHER THING...

The life of a gladiator in Britain wasn't much better than a highly-prized slave. Not many gladiators would survive more than ten matches, and few would ever live longer than 30 years old. It's thought that up to one million gladiators may have been killed in contests across the Roman Empire. Such 'sport' was popular in Roman Britain, when contests would often begin with the execution of prisoners, who were thrown to the lions, tigers or bears. The cheering crowd would go wild as the gladiators were paraded around before the fight.

Gladiators were chosen from young criminals, enemy soldiers or enslaved people, and trained in different styles of fighting to maximise their entertainment value. They learnt how to aim their swords at the major arteries of an opponent from a very young age.

FOUL FANATICS

If a gladiator was killed, the crowd would go WILD! There would often be a rush of sick people who would try to drink the dead gladiator's blood and nibble on his liver. They thought they could absorb the gladiator's vigour in this way, making them fit and strong. But that's not all. Some women collected the sweat and dead skin scrapings from gladiators and worked them into a facial cream, believing it had anti-ageing properties. It was rubbed all over the woman's face in the hope it would make her look youthful. DEAD ROMANtic (get it?).

DID YOU KNOW?

The Romans had other weird medicinal beliefs. When they weren't swigging gladiator blood, some gulped down a sweet energy drink containing goat dung. Charioteers were known to boil goat dung and vinegar into a drink or grind it into a powder. They gulped it down as a pick-me-up when they were exhausted. In fact, one of the most well-known lovers of goat dung refreshment was the crazy Emperor Nero. He must have had revoltingly bad breath!

The Romans could be very vicious,
Swordfighters were tough
and ambitious.
It was 'kill or be killed'
So if they weren't skilled
They'd be served up on toast -
how delicious!

ROMAN MEDICINE

In fact, the Romans had some pretty grim medicine. Check out some of their disgusting 'cures' for injuries below:

1 Slap a cobweb on a wound to stop the bleeding.

2 Rub tar and animal urine on the head to cure baldness.

3 Slap a nice piece of liver on the eyes if they get sore.

OUUCHH!

4 Kiss a mule's nostrils to stop hiccups (your hiccups, not the mule's).

5 If in doubt, chew a lump of garlic and dribble all that garlic-spit on any sore areas.

Surgeon, should I get him an IV?

Four what?

GROSS LIMERICK

If Romans ate more than their fill,
Clogged up their insides
and fell ill,
They had lots of potions
To loosen their motions...
Or, if push came to shove,
a huge drill!

Romans did indeed use drills to remove diseased bits of bone, to cut through the skull for basic brain surgery and to remove weapons stuck in bones.

It's best not to try this yourself!

SILLY RIDDLES

Q: What do you call a Roman with a cold?

A: Julius Sneezer.

Q: Where did Julius Caesar keep his armies?

A: Up his sleevies.

Q: How did the ancient Romans cut their hair?

A: With a pair of Caesars.

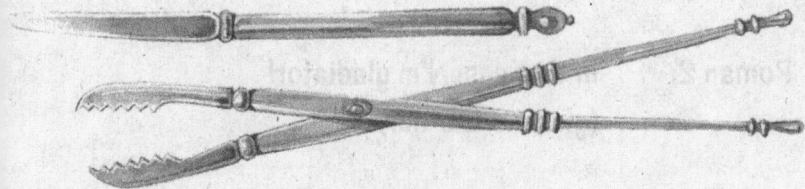

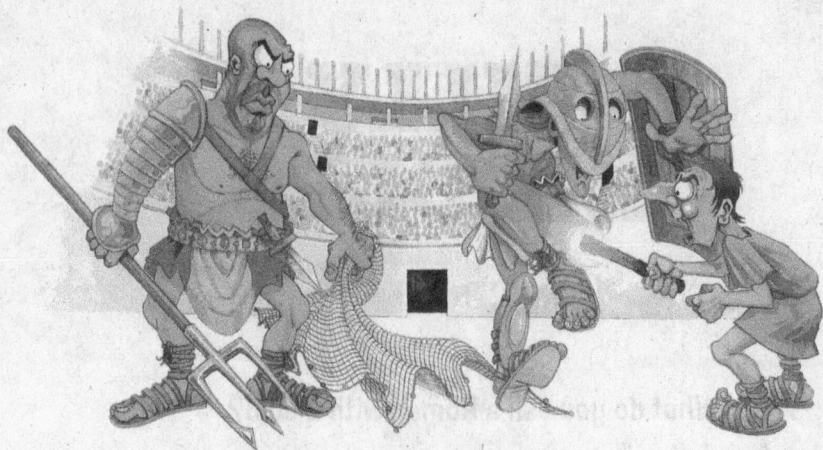

Roman I: I don't like to gossip – but I heard a rumour that Emperor Nero killed his mother.

Roman 2: I'm not surprised. She was a terrible woman and very wicked.

Roman I: He had her cooked and served up for supper.

Roman 2: In that case, I'm gladiator! (glad-he-ate-her)

Roman I: Doh!

STILL GOING STRONG

Did you hear about the gladiator who was having a rough day at the arena? His opponent had sliced off both of his arms. Nevertheless, he fought on, kicking and biting as furiously as he could. But when his opponent lopped off both feet, the gladiator had no choice but to give up. He was now both un-armed and de-feet-ed.

Despite that, I think we'd better soldier on.

I can't BEAR
to look

Decorus: Welcome to I'm A Gladiator Get Me Out of Here, where we're down to our last contestants. Today's vote will decide this year's BFG winner – The Britannia Fortunium Gadiatorus - that's the British Tournament of Gladiators. Aye, it could be quite a messy fight, right Antius?

Antius: That's right, Decorus. As always, the losers will be fed to the lions.

Decorus: Delicious! But before that, let's see what grisly
             challenges await our gladiators this week in the
             Londinium Amphitheatre Arena. And you know
             what that means?

Antius: Of course I do! Arena means 'sand' because
             that's what's on the floor (it helps to soak up the
             blood). It means we're in for some great fun –
             so long as you're not a gladiator.

Decorus: We'd better get started then.

Antius: It's time to see what's in the arena for tonight's
             show. Could it be a gladiator and a barber? Do
             you know the difference between a mad gladiator
             and his barber?

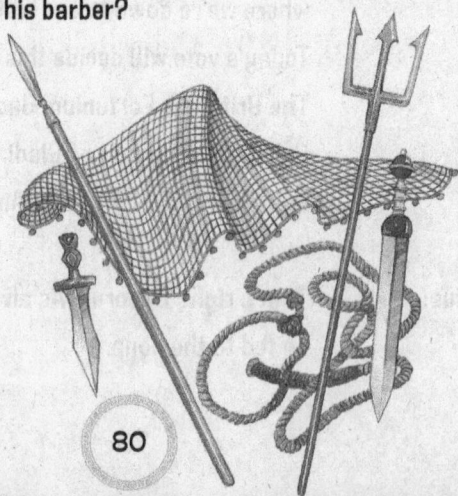

Antius:	I don't know. What is the difference between a mad gladiator and his barber?
Decorus:	One's a raving showman, the other's a shaving Roman!
Antius:	I wish I hadn't asked. Look, the gladiators are entering the arena and raising their arms...
Gladiators:	Ave, Caesar! Morituri te salutamus!
Antius:	That means 'Hail, Caesar! We who are about to die salute you!'
Decorus:	Shouldn't they also shout 'Stand and de-liver'?
Antius:	Ah yes, as some spectators like to cut out a dead gladiator's liver. Eating it is meant to make you strong and brave. Some people believe that drinking the warm blood of a dead gladiator makes you feel great.

Decorus:	Yuk. I'm glad I've got a flask of tea and a bag of chips.
Antius:	But listen up, gladiators. Here are your tasks... Your challenge will be completely armless.
Decorus:	It won't be very exciting if it's harmless.
Antius:	No, not harmless. Armless. As in unarmed – no weapons allowed.

Who wants a bear knuckle fight?

Decorus:	Got it. No weapons. No shields. No armour.
Antius:	You'll all stand in the middle of the arena totally defenceless while wild and hungry beasts are released. The audience will be gambling on which of you will last the longest.
Decorus:	The first animals you have to fight are wild bears. Big ones. You'll have a bear charging at you from the front and a bear from the behind.
Antius:	A bear behind? By the way, not many people know this, but Caesar has a giraffe which is said to be part camel, part leopard – a camelopardalis. That's true, you know.
Decorus:	Once they've dealt with the bears, there will be tigers. Big starving ones, hungry for a meal.
Antius:	The Emperor is the referee. He's about to take his seat – yikes, he's taken a tumble. Any help?
Decorus:	It's the fall of the Roman Umpire!

Antius: The gladiators may fight the bears with tridents and swords next.

Decorus: I can't BEAR the suspense, but now we've got to take a break.

Antius: We'll be back to find out what happens next.

Decorus: How will you cast your votes to decide who is this week's winner of I'm A Gladiator Get Me Out Of Here? Which one of our contestants do you think should win The Gadiatorus Maximus Prize? Er... Antius...

WAAAHHOOO!

Roar!

Antius: Yes, Decorus?

Decorus: Don't look now, but a bear has escaped and it's
                  just behind us...

Antius: Yikes! On that breaking news, we must leave you
                  with the shocking image of another bear behind.

                  (They both run off screaming.)

THE ROMANS LEAVE – AND ROME FALLS

It was the best of Thames and the worst of Thames, but it's time for us to leave Londinium.

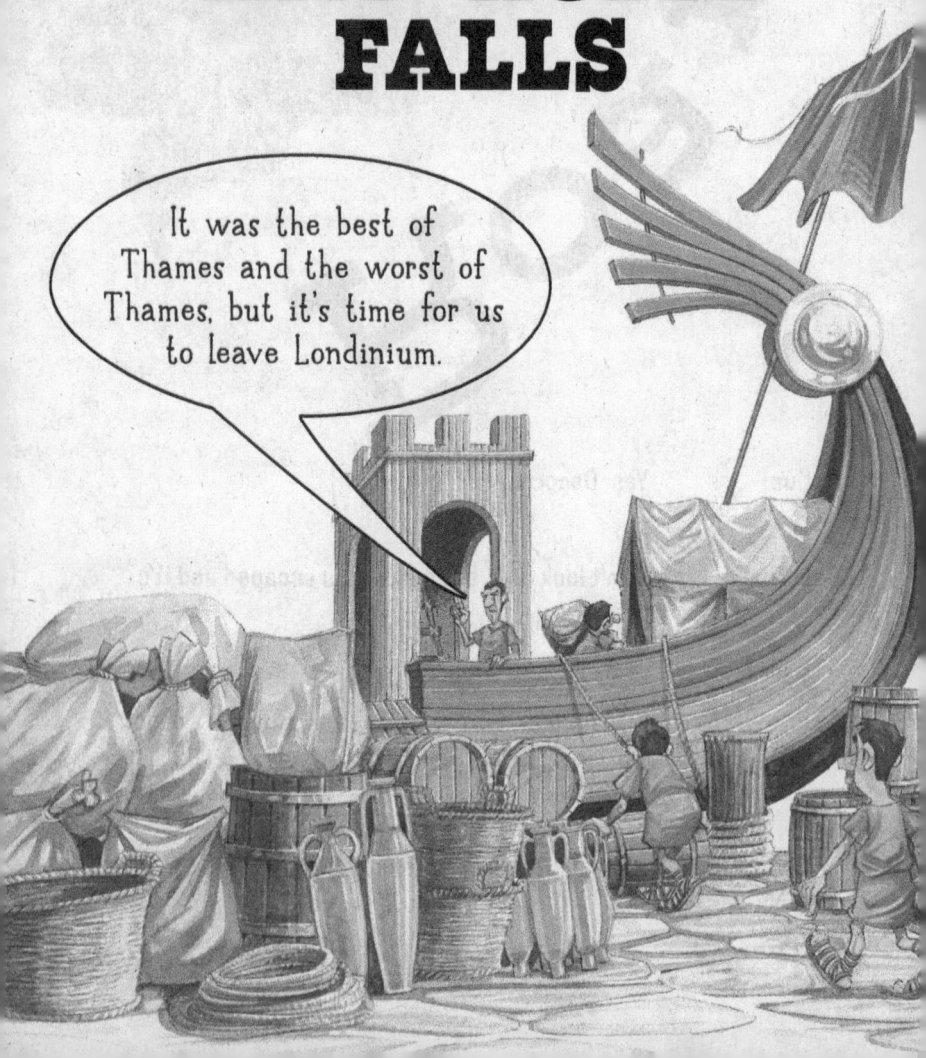

For over 350 years, Britain had been an important part of the Roman Empire. After 250 AD, the Romans were struggling to manage all their territories. Attacks from enemies outside the empire put Rome under increasing strain. By 410 AD, the Romans no longer had capacity to rule Britain – they were needed back home to defend Italy. So, the Romans finally departed, leaving the Britons to defend themselves. With no army to ward off invaders, the British people were soon attacked by other nations when the Anglo Saxons arrived. That's another story.

Why did Rome fall?

Because it slipped on some Greece!

HOW ABOUT A DATE?

The calendar we use today was started by Julius Caesar and is based on the movement of the earth around the sun, and so is called the 'solar calendar'. The solar calendar has 365 days a year, and 366 days every leap year, or every fourth year. The names of our months are taken from the names of Roman gods and rulers. The month 'July' is named after Julius Caesar, while August is named after his great nephew, the Emperor Augustus Caesar. So if your birthday is in July or August, you've got those Roman rulers to thank!

ROMAN NUMBERS

Another way the Romans helped us keep track of time was through their numberical system. You can still spot them all over the place, so keep a lookout for Roman numerals. Some people fine them a bit confusing, so just to help you out, here's all you need on the next page...

I VIII your pasta.

I'll never IV-give you.

Roman numerals

I 1	II 2	III 3	IV 4	V 5
VI 6	VII 7	VIII 8	IX 9	X 10
XI 11	XII 12	XIII 13	XIV 14	XV 15
XVI 16	XVII 17	XVIII 18	XIX 19	XX 20
XXX 30	XL 40	L 50	LX 60	LXX 70
LXXX 80	XC 90	C 100	CXXV 125	CC 200
D 500	M 1000	MM 2000	V 5000	X 10000

NUMBER FUN TIME

I, for one, understand Roman numerals. Do you, II?

A Roman walks into a bakery, holds up two fingers and says, 'I'll have five rolls please and a hot X bun.' He got IO of those!

I can't remember what 5I, 6 and 500 are in Roman numerals. That makes me LIVID.

THE ROMANS RETURN?

Just when you thought the ancient Romans left Britain for good over 1,600 years ago... they're back!

From time to time, people report seeing ghosts of Roman troops on the march along our ancient roads. Or how about this story from 1953 in York? Apparently, the ghostly troop had been spotted several times by many stunned witnesses. Yikes!

One morning in 1953, a trainee plumber called Harry Martindale was fitting new central heating pipes in the cellars of the Treasurer's House when he heard a sound like a distant trumpet. He thought it was a bit strange but carried on working up his ladder. The trumpet sounded louder and seemed to be coming closer.

Suddenly a huge cart horse emerged straight through the brick wall of the cellar! Harry fell off his ladder in shock and, as he crouched on the floor, he could clearly see the horse was being ridden by a Roman soldier. More soldiers followed, all dressed in green tunics and plumed helmets, carrying short swords and spears. At first it seemed as if they were on their knees but then they reached an excavated area, where they were walking on the old Roman road buried below the surface.

Harry scrambled frantically up the cellar steps to the ground floor. Here he was met by the house's curator who said, 'You've seen the Roman soldiers, haven't you?'

TIMELINE

(Year AD)

43 The Roman Emperor Claudius orders four legions to conquer Britain (A full strength legion was officially made up of 6,000 soldiers called legionnaires.)

48 The Romans have now conquered all territory between the Humber Estuary and the Severn Estuary. Parts that remain under British control are Wales, Scotland and the North West of England.

60 The Romans attack the Druid stronghold of Anglesey.

61 Boudicca leads a rebellion of the East Anglican Iceni tribe against the Romans. After burning down Colchester, London and St Albans, Boudicca is eventually defeated at the Battle of Watling Street.

80 London has grown into a large town with a forum, basilica, governor's palace and even an amphitheatre.

84 The Romans head further north to battle with the Caledonians in Scotland.

100 Most of the 8,000 miles of Roman roads in Britain are completed, allowing troops and goods to travel easily across the country.

Timeline continued
(Year AD)

122   To strengthen the border between Roman-occupied Britain and Scotland, Emperor Hadrian orders the building of a wall.

139 – 140   The Antonine Wall in Scotland is built, moving the northern border of Roman-occupied Britain.

150   Villas start appearing across the British countryside, some with mosaic floors.

209   After years of conflict with the northern tribes, the Romans lead an army to Hadrian's Wall border to sort out the Caledonians. Eventually peace treaties are signed.

211 Britain is split into two provinces; the south to be called 'Britannia Superior' (as it's closer to Rome), with the north being named 'Britannia Inferior'. London is the new capital of the south, with York the capital of the north.

I'll pay you with a pinch of salt. (Yes, Romans did this.)

Timeline continued
(Year AD)

250 onwards
New threats to Britannia emerge as the Scottish Picts, as well as the Angles, Saxons and Jutes from Germany and Scandinavia, threaten Roman lands.

255
With increasing external danger, London's city wall is finished with the final stretch along the north bank of the Thames.

287
The admiral of the Roman Channel fleet, Carausius, declares himself Emperor of Britain and starts minting his own coins.

314
Christianity becomes legal in the Roman Empire.

367
Barbarians from Scotland, Ireland and Germany launch raids on Roman Britain. Many towns are plundered and Britain falls into disorder.

396 Large-scale Barbarian attacks on Britain start up again.

399 Peace is fully restored throughout Roman Britannia.

406 With the Roman Empire focused on serious threats to Italy, reinforcements have stopped and Britain is left to fend for herself.

410 With increased attacks from the Saxons, Scots, Picts and Angles, Britain turns to the Roman Emperor Honorius for help. He writes back, refusing to send any help. This letter marked the end of Roman Britain. The Romans return to Rome, and the great empire crumbles within 66 years.

AND FINALLY...

No, not underpants but a subligaculum! This was a kind of underwear worn by ancient Romans. It could be a bit like a pair of shorts, or a simple loincloth, and was worn by men and women. It was part of the dress of gladiators, athletes and of actors on the stage (but a bit draughty in those chilly British winters). So just remember... never get your subligaculum in a twist.

THE ROMAN RIOT QUIZ

I. What does the Greek word 'keltoi' mean?

a) Hairy

b) Barbarian

c) Dangerous

2. In what year was the Roman emperor Romulus Augustus defeated by the German Goth Odoacer?

a) 476 AD

b) 385 AD

c) 1997 AD

Have you seen the dormouse pasta?

3. What is the name of the bluish dye native Britons painted themselves with?

a) Woad

b) Alizarin

c) Cresyl

4. What language did Romans speak and write?

a) Welsh

b) Italian

c) Latin

5. **What did Romans use to wipe their bottoms?**

a) Andrex

b) Stray cats

c) A sponge on a stick

6. What did 'Britannia' mean in Latin?

a) Land of spray tans

b) Land of tin

c) Land of terrible weather

7. Who led the Celtic tribes against the Roman invaders in 60 AD?

a) Queen Boudicca

b) King Canute

c) Alfred the Great

8. What did the audience sometimes do when a gladiator was killed?

a) Try to give CPR

b) Drink his blood

c) Get a selfie with the corpse

These questions are far too silly!

Fighting you is child's play!

9. Which Roman emperor built a wall across the north of England to keep out the Picts?

a) Hadrian

b) Augustus

c) Julian

10. What was the name for a warm Roman bath?

a) Jacuzzi

b) Frigidarium

c) Tepidarium

GLOSSARY

Amphitheatre: an open-air venue used for entertainment.

Aqueduct: a bridge-like, man-made channel system used to transport water from one location to another.

Archaeologist: a person who studies excavated sites and artefacts to find out about past civilisations.

Barbarian: a person who lived outside of the Roman Empire. The Romans believed they were violent and uncivilised people.

Boudicca: a warrior queen of the ancient British Iceni tribe. She wreaked havoc against the Romans and lead a fierce-but-failed uprising in AD 60-61.

Britons: the native people of Britain who lived on the island before the arrival of the Romans and, later, the Anglo-Saxons.

Colosseum: a giant, oval ampitheatre located in Rome that was mainly used for gladiator fights.

Emperor: the supreme ruler and head of the Roman Empire.

Gladiator: a warrior trained to fight against other gladiators or animals for entertainment in the ampitheatre. Many were enslaved people.

Goths: a Germanic people from Scandinavia who frequently attacked and engaged in warfare with the Roman Empire.

Julius Caesar: Roman general and dictator who ruled the Roman Empire until his assassination in 44 BC.

Latin: the ancient language the Romans spoke.

Legion: a military unit around 5,000 men strong, recruited from Rome's citizens.

Londinium: the Roman name for London.

Mosaic: a picture or pattern made by sticking together lots of small pieces of tile, stone or glass.

Picts: an ancient group of people from what is now eastern and north-eastern Scotland. They were known as 'the painted ones' and heavily rebelled against Roman rule.

Republic: a country without a king, queen or emperor. Instead, the state's supreme ruler is elected by the people.

Villa: a large country house, formed of farm and domestic buildings around a central courtyard.

GIGGLE GURU

I tickled my brain with Roman rib-ticklers, hilarious history,
and silly stories. Having conquered the quiz,
I'm now a proven pro on all things Roman!

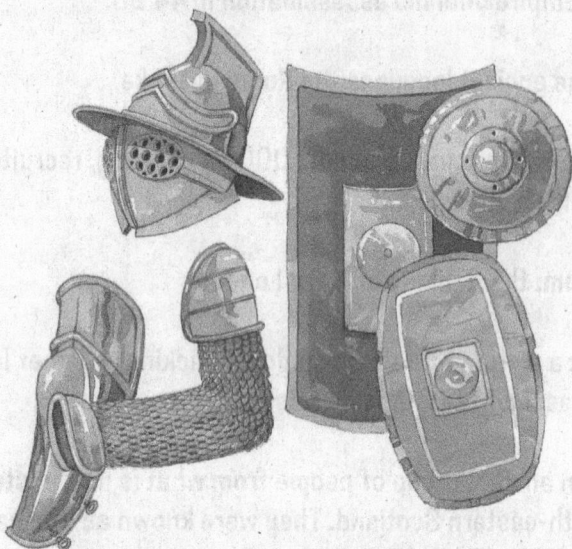

Name:

....

Date:

........../ ..../ ....